Table of contents

Abstract ....

Introduction 3

1   Basic Concepts: Variables, Conditions, and Loops 5

   1.1   Exercises 5

   1.2   Correction 7

2   Lists, Functions, and Lambda Functions 12

   2.1   Exercises 12

      2.1.1   Functions 12

      2.1.2   Lists 12

      2.1.3   Lambda Functions 13

   2.2   Correction 14

      2.2.1   Functions 14

      2.2.2   Lists 15

      2.2.3   Lambda functions 21

3   Strings 24

   3.1   Exercises 24

   3.2   Correction 26

4   Dictionaries, Tuples, and Sets 32

   4.1   Exercises 32

      4.1.1   Dictionaries 32

      4.1.2   Tuples 33

      4.1.3   Sets 33

   4.2   Correction 35

      4.2.1   Dictionaries 35

      4.2.2   Tuples 37

      4.2.3   Sets 38

5   Files 41

   5.1   Exercises 41

   5.2   Correction 43

6   Recursion 49

   6.1   Exercises 49

   6.2   Correction 51

7   Practice exercise (Data structures) 54

   7.1   Exercise 54

7.2   Correction 55

Abstract

This book is a comprehensive guide to learning Python programming, designed to support students in developing their programming skills. By following this guide and completing the exercises, readers will develop a strong foundation in Python programming and gain confidence in tackling programming challenges. Whether you are a beginner or an experienced programmer, this book serves as a valuable resource for mastering Python and advancing your programming abilities.

The book is divided into seven chapters:

Chapter 1: Variables, Conditions, and Loops

Chapter 2: Functions, Lists, and Lambda Functions

Chapter 3: Strings

Chapter 4: Dictionaries, Tuples, and Sets

Chapter 5: Files

Chapter 6: Recursion

Chapter 7: Practice Exercise (Data Structures)

Introduction

This book is designed to provide you with a series of structured and solved exercises that will help you better understand the fundamental concepts of programming. Drawing from our experience in the field of programming, particularly with Python, we have ensured that the content of this book is progressive, coherent, and clear.

The chapters in this book cover the fundamental concepts and syntax of Python, following a pedagogical approach. In Chapter 1, you will explore the basics of programming, such as variables, conditions, and loops. Chapter 2 introduces lists and functions, while Chapter 3 focuses on string manipulation. Chapter 4 covers tuples, sets and dictionaries. In Chapter 5, you will study file handling. Chapter 6 explores the concept of recursion. Lastly, Chapter 7 offers practical exercise on data structures.

Python is a feature-rich language that facilitates operations on lists and strings. In this book, we provide two versions of exercise solutions: one without the use of built-in functions and another with the use of built-in functions. The goal is to allow you to practice developing algorithms to solve specific problems.

This book is intended for anyone looking to learn or deepen their knowledge of Python. It is designed to accompany you on your learning journey. We hope that within these pages, you will find the tools and knowledge necessary to develop your programming skills.

Chapter 1

Basic Concepts: Variables, Conditions, and Loops

1 Basic Concepts: Variables, Conditions, and Loops

1.1 Exercises

Exercise 1.1

Write a program that asks the user to enter a number and displays whether the number is even or odd.

Exercise 1.2

Write a program that asks the user to enter two numbers and displays the larger of the two.

Exercise 1.3

Write a program that asks the user to enter their age and displays whether they are of legal age or a minor (considering the legal age to be 18 years old).

Exercise 1.4

Write a program that asks the user to enter a grade out of 20 and displays their mention based on the grade (for example, "Excellent" for a grade greater than or equal to 16, "Good" for a grade between 14 and 16, etc.).

Exercise 1.5

Write a program that asks the user to enter three lengths and checks if these lengths can form a triangle. If they can, display "The lengths can form a triangle"; otherwise, display "The lengths cannot form a triangle".

Exercise 1.6

Write a program that calculates x raised to the power of n, where n is a positive integer.

Exercise 1.7

Write a program that calculates the factorial of a given positive integer n.

Input: n (a natural number)

Output: factorial(n) = 1 * 2 * 3 * ... * (n-1) * n

Exercise 1.8

Write a program that determines whether an integer n is prime.

Exercise 1.9

Write a program that determines whether a number is perfect.

Reminder: A number is perfect if it is equal to the sum of its divisors.

Example: 6 is a perfect number: $6 = 1 + 2 + 3$

Exercise 1.10

Write a program that determines the first integer N for which the sum of numbers from 1 to N strictly exceeds 100.

Exercise 1.11

Write a program that finds the smallest prime number greater than a given positive integer n.

1.2 Correction

Exercise 1.1:

```python
number = int(input("Enter a number: "))
if number % 2 == 0:
    print("The number is even.")
else:
    print("The number is odd.")
```

Exercise 1.2:

```python
number1 = int(input("Enter the first number: "))
number2 = int(input("Enter the second number: "))
if number1 > number2:
    print("The larger number is:", number1)
else:
    print("The larger number is:", number2)
```

Exercise 1.3:

```python
age = int(input("Enter your age: "))
if age >= 18:
    print("You are of legal age.")
else:
    print("You are a minor.")
```

Exercise 1.4:

```python
grade = int(input("Enter your grade out of 20: "))
if grade >= 16:
    print("Excellent")
elif grade >= 14:
    print("Good")
elif grade >= 12:
    print("Fairly good")
```

```python
elif grade >= 10:
    print("Pass")
else:
    print("Insufficient")
```

Exercise 1.5 :

```python
a = float(input("Enter the first length: "))
b = float(input("Enter the second length: "))
c = float(input("Enter the third length: "))
if a + b > c and a + c > b and b + c > a:
    print("The lengths can form a triangle.")
else:
    print("The lengths cannot form a triangle.")
```

Exercise 1.6 :

```python
x = float(input("Enter the value of x: "))
n = int(input("Enter the value of n: "))
result = 1
for i in range(n):
    result *= x
print("The result of", x, "raised to the power of", n, "is:", result)
```

Exercise 1.7:

```python
n = int(input("Enter a natural number: "))
factorial = 1
for i in range(1, n + 1):
    factorial *= i
print("The factorial of", n, "is:", factorial)
```

Exercise 1.8:

```python
n = int(input("Enter an integer: "))
if n <= 1:
    print(n, "is not prime.")
```

```python
    else:
        is_prime = True
        for i in range(2, int(n ** 0.5) + 1):
            if n % i == 0:
                is_prime = False
                break
        if is_prime:
            print(n, "is prime.")
        else:
            print(n, "is not prime.")
```

Exercise 1.9 :

```python
number = int(input("Enter a number: "))
sum_of_divisors = 0
for i in range(1, number):
    if number % i == 0:
        sum_of_divisors += i
if sum_of_divisors == number:
    print(number, "is a perfect number.")
else:
    print(number, "is not a perfect number.")
```

Exercise 1.10:

```python
sum = 0
N = 1
while sum <= 100:
    N += 1
    sum += N


print("The first integer N for which the sum from 1 to N strictly exceeds 100 is:", N)
```

Exercise 1.11:

```python
n = int(input("Enter a positive integer: "))
```

```python
number = n + 1
while True:
    is_prime = True
    for i in range(2, int(number ** 0.5) + 1):
        if number % i == 0:
            is_prime = False
            break
    if is_prime:
        break
    number += 1
print("The smallest prime number strictly greater than", n, "is:", number)
```

Chapter 2

Lists and Functions, and Lambda Functions

2 Lists, Functions, and Lambda Functions

2.1 Exercises

2.1.1 Functions

Note: The solutions are presented with an example of functions testing.

Exercise 2.1.1

Provide the function that calculates the maximum of three values a, b, and c given as parameters.

Exercise 2.1.2

Provide the function that calculates the area and perimeter of a rectangle.

Exercise 2.1.3

Provide the function that swaps two values a and b given as parameters.

2.1.2 Lists

Note: Python offers many built-in functions that simplify list manipulations. In this book, we provide an approach without using the predefined functions and an approach that incorporates them.

Exercise 2.2.1

Provide the function that allows entering a list of n values.

Exercise 2.2.2

Write a program that searches for the value x in a list L of N elements (Sequential search).

Exercise 2.2.3

Given a list of integers, remove the null elements from the list.

Exercise 2.2.4

Write a program that allows entering 10 integers into a list, then searches and displays the minimum and maximum values entered in the list. The display will also mention the indices where the minimum and maximum values are located.

Exercise 2.2.5 (Selection Sort)

Provide the program that sorts a list of n elements using selection sort.

Principle: We search for the smallest element in the list and place it first, then start from the second element while ignoring the first one and search for the smallest element in the remaining list to place it second, and so on. At the end of n passes, the list is sorted.

Exercise 2.2.6

Write a program that checks if a list L of length n is sorted.

Hint: L is sorted if L[i] <=L[i+1] for i ranging from 0 to n-2.

Exercise 2.2.7

Given a list L of positive and negative integers, place the negative elements at the beginning of the list.

Exercise 2.2.8

Provide the function that reads a list of length n and displays the number of even integers contained in that list.

Exercise 2.2.9

Provide a function that inserts a value v at index i in a list of length n.

Exercise 2.2.10

Provide a function that reverses the elements of a list.

2.1.3 Lambda Functions

Exercise 2.3.1

Write a lambda function that takes an integer as input and returns the square of that number.

Exercise 2.3.2

Write a lambda function that takes two numbers as input and returns their sum.

Exercise 2.3.3

Write a lambda function that takes a string as input and returns the length of that string.

Exercise 2.3.4

Write a lambda function that takes a list of numbers as input and returns the list sorted in ascending order.

2.2 Correction

2.2.1 Functions

Exercise 2.1

```python
def maximum(a, b, c):
    max_value = max(a, b, c)
    return max_value
# Test
a = 5
b = 10
c = 3
print(maximum(a, b, c))  # Expected output: 10
```

Exercise 2.2

```python
def rectangle_properties(length, width):
    area = length * width
    perimeter = 2 * (length + width)
    return area, perimeter
# Test
length = 4
width = 6
surface, perimeter = rectangle_properties(length, width)
print("Surface:", surface)  # Expected output: 24
print("Perimeter:", perimeter)  # Expected output: 20
```

Exercise 2.3

```python
def swap_values(a, b):
    temp = a
    a = b
    b = temp
    return a, b
```

```python
# Test
a = 10
b = 5
a, b = swap_values(a, b)
print("a =", a)  # Expected output: 5
print("b =", b)  # Expected output: 10
```

2.2.2 Lists

Exercise 2.2.1
```python
def input_values(n):
    values = []
    for i in range(n):
        value = input("Enter a value: ")
        values.append(value)
    return values
# Test
n = 3
value_list = input_values(n)
print(value_list)  # Example input: 1, 2, 3 -> Expected output: ['1', '2', '3']
```

Exercise 2.2.2 (Sequential Search) - With built-in functions
```python
list = [2, 5, 8, 10, 12]
value = 8
if value in list:
    print("The value", value, "was found in the list.")
else:
    print("The value", value, "was not found in the list.")
```

Exercise 2.2.2 (Sequential Search) - Without built-in functions
```python
def sequential_search(L, x):
    for i in range(len(L)):
        if L[i] == x:
```

```python
        return True
    return False
# Test
list = [2, 5, 8, 10, 12]
value = 8
if sequential_search(list, value):
    print("The value", value, "was found in the list.")
else:
    print("The value", value, "was not found in the list.")
```

Exercise 2.2.3 - With built-in functions
```python
list = [2, 0, 5, 0, 8, 0, 10, 0]
list = [element for element in list if element != 0]
print("List after removing zero elements:", list)
```

Exercise 2.2.3 - Without built-in functions
```python
def remove_zero_elements(L):
    i = 0
    while i < len(L):
        if L[i] == 0:
            L.pop(i)
        else:
            i += 1
# Test
list = [2, 0, 5, 0, 8, 0, 10, 0]
remove_zero_elements(list)
print("List after removing zero elements:", list)
```

Exercise 2.2.4 - With built-in functions
```python
numbers = []
for i in range(10):
    number = int(input("Enter an integer number: "))
    numbers.append(number)
```

```python
min_val = min(numbers)
min_index = numbers.index(min_val)
max_val = max(numbers)
max_index = numbers.index(max_val)
print("The minimum value is", min_val, "at index", min_index)
print("The maximum value is", max_val, "at index", max_index)
```

Exercise 2.2.4 - Without built-in functions

```python
def find_min_max(list):
    min_val = list[0]
    max_val = list[0]
    min_index = 0
    max_index = 0
    for i in range(1, len(list)):
        if list[i] < min_val:
            min_val = list[i]
            min_index = i
        if list[i] > max_val:
            max_val = list[i]
            max_index = i
    return min_val, min_index, max_val, max_index
numbers = []
for i in range(10):
    number = int(input("Enter an integer number: "))
    numbers.append(number)
min_val, min_index, max_val, max_index = find_min_max(numbers)
print("The minimum value is", min_val, "at index", min_index)
print("The maximum value is", max_val, "at index", max_index)
```

Exercise 2.2.5 (Selection Sort) - Without built-in functions

```python
def selection_sort(list):
    for i in range(len(list)):
        min_index = i
```

```python
        for j in range(i + 1, len(list)):
            if list[j] < list[min_index]:
                min_index = j
        list[i], list[min_index] = list[min_index], list[i]
# Test
numbers = [5, 2, 8, 3, 10, 1]
selection_sort(numbers)
print("Sorted list:", numbers)
```

Exercise 2.2.5 (Python Sort) - With built-in functions

```python
numbers = [5, 2, 8, 3, 10, 1]
numbers.sort()
print("Sorted list:", numbers)
```

Exercise 2.2.6 - With built-in functions

```python
numbers = [1, 2, 3, 5, 4, 6]
if numbers == sorted(numbers):
    print("The list is sorted.")
else:
    print("The list is not sorted.")
```

Exercise 2.2.6 - Without built-in functions

```python
def is_sorted(list):
    for i in range(len(list) - 1):
        if list[i] > list[i + 1]:
            return False
    return True
numbers = [1, 2, 3, 5, 4, 6]
if is_sorted(numbers):
    print"The list is sorted."
else:
    print("The list is not sorted.")
```

Exercise 2.2.7 - With built-in functions

```python
numbers = [2, -3, 5, -1, -8, 4, -6]
numbers.sort(key=lambda x: x >= 0)
print("List after placing negative elements at the beginning:", numbers)
```

Exercise 2.2.7 - Without built-in functions

```python
def place_negatives_start(list):
    i = 0
    j = len(list) - 1
    while i < j:
        if list[i] < 0:
            i += 1
        elif list[j] >= 0:
            j -= 1
        else:
            list[i], list[j] = list[j], list[i]
            i += 1
            j -= 1
# Test
numbers = [2, -3, 5, -1, -8, 4, -6]
place_negatives_start(numbers)
print("List after placing negative elements at the beginning:", numbers)
```

Exercise 2.2.8 - With built-in functions

```python
def count_even_numbers(L, n):
    count = sum(1 for num in L if num % 2 == 0)
    return count
# Test
L = [1, 2, 3, 4, 5, 6, 7, 8, 9, 10]
n = len(L)
print(count_even_numbers(L, n))  # Expected output: 5
```

Exercise 2.2.8 - Without built-in functions

```python
def count_even_numbers(L, n):
    count = 0
    for i in range(n):
        if L[i] % 2 == 0:
            count += 1
    return count
# Test
L = [1, 2, 3, 4, 5, 6, 7, 8, 9, 10]
n = len(L)
print(count_even_numbers(L, n))  # Expected output: 5
```

Exercise 2.2.9 - With built-in functions

```python
def insert(L, n, i, v):
    L.insert(i, v)
# Test
L= [1, 2, 3, 4, 5]
n = len(L)
i = 2
v = 10
insert(L, n, i, v)
print(L)  # Expected output: [1, 2, 10, 3, 4, 5]
```

Exercise 2.2.9 - Without built-in functions

```python
def insert(L, n, i, v):
    L.append(0)  # Add an empty space at the end of the list
    for j in range(n, i, -1):
        L[j] = L[j-1]
    L[i] = v
# Test
L = [1, 2, 3, 4, 5]
n = len(L)
i = 2
```

```
v = 10
insert(L, n, i, v)
print(L)  # Expected output: [1, 2, 10, 3, 4, 5]
```

Exercise 2.2.10 - With built-in functions

```
def reverse_list(L):
    return L[::-1]
# Test
L = [1, 2, 3, 4, 5]
reversed_list = reverse_list(L)
print(reversed_list)  # Expected output: [5, 4, 3, 2, 1]
```

Exercise 2.2.10 - Without built-in functions

```
def reverse_list(L):
    n = len(L)
    for i in range(n//2):
        L[i], L[n-i-1] = L[n-i-1], L[i]
    return L
# Test
L = [1, 2, 3, 4, 5]
reversed_list = reverse_list(L)
print(reversed_list)  # Expected output: [5, 4, 3, 2, 1]
```

2.2.3   Lambda functions

Exercise 2.3.1

```
square = lambda x: x**2
# Test:
print(square(4))  # Expected output: 16
print(square(-2))  # Expected output: 4
```

Exercise 2.3.2

```
sum_func = lambda x, y: x + y
```

```python
# Test:
print(sum_func(2, 3))  # Expected output: 5
print(sum_func(-1, 7))  # Expected output: 6
```

Exercise 2.3.3

```python
length = lambda string: len(string)
# Test:
print(length("Bonjour"))  # Expected output: 7
print(length("Hello, World!"))  # Expected output: 13
```

Exercise 2.3.4

```python
ascending_sort = lambda list: sorted(list)
# Test:
print(ascending_sort([3, 1, 4, 2]))  # Expected output: [1, 2, 3, 4]
print(ascending_sort([-1, 0, 10, -5]))  # Expected output: [-5, -1, 0, 10]
```

Chapter 3

Strings

3 Strings

3.1 Exercises

Note: Python offers many functionalities that simplify string manipulations. In this book, we present two approaches: one without using built-in functions and one that incorporates them. The solutions are presented with an example of function testing.

Exercise 3.1

Write a function that calculates the length of a string. The function returns the length of the string.

Exercise 3.2

1) Write a function `search_char` that returns the position of the first occurrence of the character `c` (the character passed as an argument) in a string `s`. If this character does not appear in the string, the function returns -1.

2) Give a function `count_char` that takes a string `s` and a character `c` as parameters, and counts the number of occurrences of `c` in `s`.

Exercise 3.3

Write a function that removes spaces from a string `ch`.

Exercise 3.4

Write a function that checks if a string `ch2` is included in a string `ch1`. The function takes both strings as parameters. The function returns 1 if `ch2` is included in `ch1`, otherwise it returns 0.

Exercise 3.5

Give a function that concatenates two strings. The function takes both strings as parameters.

Exercise 3.6

Give a function that compares two strings. The function returns 1 if the two strings are equal, otherwise it returns 0. The function takes both strings as parameters.

Exercise 3.7:

Write a program that asks the user to enter a sentence containing multiple words separated by spaces. Then, use the `split()` function to split the sentence into individual words and display them one by one.

Exercise 3.8:

Write a program that asks the user to enter a series of numbers separated by commas. Then, use the `split()` function to separate the numbers and convert them into a list of integers. Finally, display the list of numbers.

3.2 Correction

Exercise 3.1 - Without Built-in Functions:

```python
def get_string_length(ch):
    count = 0
    for char in ch:
        count += 1
    return count
# Test
ch = "Hello, world!"
print(get_string_length(ch))  # Expected output: 13
```

Exercise 3.1 - With Built-in Functions:

```python
def get_string_length(ch):
    return len(ch)
# Test
ch = "Hello, world!"
print(get_string_length(ch))  # Expected output: 13
```

Exercise 3.2 (1) - Without Built-in Functions:

```python
def find_character(s, c):
    for i in range(len(s)):
        if s[i] == c:
            return i
    return -1
# Test
s = "Hello, world!"
c = "o"
print(find_character(s, c))  # Expected output: 4
```

Exercise 3.2 (1) - With Built-in Functions:

```python
def find_character(s, c):
```

```python
    return s.find(c)


# Test the find_character function
s = "Hello, world!"
c = "o"
print(find_character(s, c))  # Expected output: 4
```

Exercise 3.2 (2) - Without Built-in Functions:

```python
def count_character(s, c):
    count = 0
    for char in s:
        if char == c:
            count += 1
    return count
# Test
s = "Hello, world!"
c = "l"
print(count_character(s, c))  # Expected output: 3
```

Exercise 3.2 (2) - With Built-in Functions:

```python
def count_character(s, c):
    return s.count(c)
# Test
s = "Hello, world!"
c = "l"
print(count_character(s, c))  # Expected output: 3
```

Exercise 3.3 - Without Built-in Functions:

```python
def remove_spaces(ch):
    ch_without_spaces = ""
    for char in ch:
        if char != " ":
            ch_without_spaces += char
```

```python
    return ch_without_spaces


# Test
ch = "Hello, world!"
print(remove_spaces(ch))  # Expected output: "Hello,world!"
```

Exercise 3.3 - With Built-in Functions:

```python
def remove_spaces(ch):
    return ch.replace(" ", "")
# Test
ch = "Hello, world!"
print(remove_spaces(ch))  # Expected output: "Hello,world!"
```

Exercise 3.4 - Without Built-in Functions:

```python
def check_inclusion(ch1, ch2):
    ch1_len = len(ch1)
    ch2_len = len(ch2)
    for i in range(ch1_len - ch2_len + 1):
        if ch1[i:i+ch2_len] == ch2:
            return 1
    return 0
# Test
ch1 = "Hello, world!"
ch2 = "world"
print(check_inclusion(ch1, ch2))  # Expected output: 1
```

Exercise 3.4 - With Built-in Functions:

```python
def check_inclusion(ch1, ch2):
    return ch2 in ch1
# Test
ch1 = "Hello, world!"
ch2 = "world"
print(check_inclusion(ch1, ch2))  # Expected output: 1
```

Exercise 3.5 - Without Built-in Functions:

```python
def concatenate_strings(ch1, ch2):
    return ch1 + ch2
# Test
ch1 = "Hello"
ch2 = " world!"
print(concatenate_strings(ch1, ch2))  # Expected output: "Hello world!"
```

Exercise 3.5 - With Built-in Functions:

```python
def concatenate_strings(ch1, ch2):
    return "".join([ch1, ch2])
# Test
ch1 = "Hello"
ch2 = " world!"
print(concatenate_strings(ch1, ch2))  # Expected output: "Hello world!"
```

Exercise 3.6 - Without Built-in Functions:

```python
def compare_strings(ch1, ch2):
    if len(ch1) != len(ch2):
        return 0
    for i in range(len(ch1)):
        if ch1[i] != ch2[i]:
            return 0
    return 1
# Test
ch1 = "Hello"
ch2 = "Hello"
print(compare_strings(ch1, ch2))  # Expected output: 1
```

Exercise 3.6 - With Built-in Functions:

```python
def compare_strings(ch1, ch2):
    return ch1 == ch2
```

```python
# Test
ch1 = "Hello"
ch2 = "Hello"
print(compare_strings(ch1, ch2))  # Expected output: 1
```

Exercise 3.7 :

```python
sentence = input("Enter a sentence: ")
words = sentence.split()
for word in words:
    print(word)
# Output:
# Enter a sentence: Hello, how are you?
# Hello,
# how
# are
# you?
```

```python
# Exercise 3.8:
numbers_str = input("Enter numbers separated by commas: ")
numbers_list = numbers_str.split(",")
numbers = [int(num) for num in numbers_list]
print(numbers)
# Output:
# Enter numbers separated by commas: 1, 2, 3, 4, 5
# [1, 2, 3, 4, 5]
```

Chapter 4

Dictionaries, Tuples, and Sets

4 Dictionaries, Tuples, and Sets

4.1 Exercises

4.1.1 Dictionaries

Exercise 4.1.1

Write a function that counts the number of elements in a dictionary. The function should take the dictionary as a parameter and return the number of elements.

Exercise 4.1.2

Write a function that merges two dictionaries into one. The function should take the two dictionaries as parameters and return the merged dictionary.

Exercise 4.1.3

Write a function that finds the key corresponding to a given value in a dictionary. The function should take the dictionary and the desired value as parameters, and return the corresponding key.

Exercise 4.1.4

Write a function that checks if all the keys in a dictionary are present in a given list. The function should take the dictionary and the list as parameters, and return True if all the keys are present, otherwise False.

Exercise 4.1.5

Write a function that calculates the sum of the values in a dictionary. The function should take the dictionary as a parameter and return the sum of the values.

Exercise 4.1.6

Write a function that finds the maximum value in a dictionary. The function should take the dictionary as a parameter and return the maximum value.

Exercise 4.1.7

Write a function that finds the key corresponding to the maximum value in a dictionary. The function should take the dictionary as a parameter and return the corresponding key.

Exercise 4.1.8

Write a function that removes an element from a dictionary using its key. The function should take the dictionary and the key to be removed as parameters, and modify the dictionary accordingly.

4.1.2   Tuples

Exercise 4.2.1

Write a function that calculates the sum of the elements in an integer tuple. The function should take the tuple as a parameter and return the sum.

Exercise 4.2.2

Write a function that finds the maximum element in a tuple. The function should take the tuple as a parameter and return the maximum element.

Exercise 4.2.3

Write a function that reverses the order of elements in a tuple. The function should take the tuple as a parameter and return a new tuple with the reversed elements.

Exercise 4.2.4

Write a function that counts the number of occurrences of an element in a tuple. The function should take the tuple and the element to be searched as parameters, and return the number of occurrences.

Exercise 4.2.5

Write a function that merges two tuples into one. The function should take the two tuples as parameters and return the merged tuple.

Exercise 4.2.6

Write a function that extracts a subsequence from a tuple by specifying a start index and an end index. The function should take the tuple, the start index, and the end index as parameters, and return a new tuple with the extracted subsequence.

4.1.3   Sets

Exercise 4.3.1

Write a function that takes two sets as input and returns a new set containing the common elements between the two sets.

Exercise 4.3.2

Write a function that takes two sets as input and returns a new set containing the unique elements from both sets.

Exercise 4.3.3

Write a function that takes a set as input and returns the length of the set.

Exercise 4.3.4

Write a function that takes two sets as input and returns a new set containing the elements that are present in the first set but not in the second set.

Exercise 4.3.5

Write a function that takes two sets as input and returns a new set containing the elements that are present in either of the two sets, but not in both.

Exercise 4.3.6

Write a function that takes two sets as input and returns a new set containing the elements that are present in the first set and not in the second set, and vice versa.

4.2 Correction

4.2.1 Dictionaries

Exercise 4.1.1:

```python
def count_elements(dictionary):
    return len(dictionary)
# Test
my_dictionary = {'a': 1, 'b': 2, 'c': 3}
print(count_elements(my_dictionary)) # Expected output: 3
```

Exercise 4.1.2:

```python
def merge_dictionaries(dictionary1, dictionary2):
    merge = {**dictionary1, **dictionary2}
    return merge
# Test
dictionary1 = {'a': 1, 'b': 2}
dictionary2 = {'c': 3, 'd': 4}
print(merge_dictionaries(dictionary1, dictionary2)) # Expected output: {'a': 1, 'b': 2, 'c': 3, 'd': 4}
```

Exercise 4.1.3:

```python
def find_key(dictionary, value):
    for key, val in dictionary.items():
        if val == value:
            return key
    return None
# Test
my_dictionary = {'a': 1, 'b': 2, 'c': 3}
print(find_key(my_dictionary, 2)) # Expected output: 'b'
```

Exercise 4.1.4:

```python
def check_keys(dictionary, keys):
    return all(key in dictionary for key in keys)
# Test
```

```python
my_dictionary = {'a': 1, 'b': 2, 'c': 3}
my_keys = ['a', 'b']
print(check_keys(my_dictionary, my_keys))  # Expected output: True
```

Exercise 4.1.5:

```python
def calculate_sum_values(dictionary):
    return sum(dictionary.values())
# Test
my_dictionary = {'a': 1, 'b': 2, 'c': 3}
print(calculate_sum_values(my_dictionary))  # Expected output: 6
```

Exercise 4.1.6:

```python
def find_max_value(dictionary):
    return max(dictionary.values())
# Test
my_dictionary = {'a': 1, 'b': 2, 'c': 3}
print(find_max_value(my_dictionary))  # Expected output: 3
```

Exercise 4.1.7:

```python
def find_max_key(dictionary):
    return max(dictionary, key=dictionary.get)
# Test
my_dictionary = {'a': 1, 'b': 2, 'c': 3}
print(find_max_key(my_dictionary))  # Expected output: 'c'
```

Exercise 4.1.8:

```python
def remove_element(dictionary, key):
    if key in dictionary:
        del dictionary[key]
# Test
my_dictionary = {'a': 1, 'b': 2, 'c': 3}
remove_element(my_dictionary, 'b')
print(my_dictionary)  # Expected output: {'a': 1, 'c': 3}
```

4.2.2 Tuples

Exercise 4.2.1:

```python
def calculate_sum(tuple_of_integers):
    return sum(tuple_of_integers)
# Test
my_tuple = (1, 2, 3, 4, 5)
print(calculate_sum(my_tuple))  # Expected output: 15
```

Exercise 4.2.2:

```python
def find_max(tuple_of_elements):
    return max(tuple_of_elements)
# Test
my_tuple = (1, 5, 2, 4, 3)
print(find_max(my_tuple))  # Expected output: 5
```

Exercise 4.2.3:

```python
def reverse_tuple(tuple_of_elements):
    return tuple_of_elements[::-1]
# Test
my_tuple = (1, 2, 3, 4, 5)
print(reverse_tuple(my_tuple))  # Expected output: (5, 4, 3, 2, 1)
```

Exercise 4.2.4:

```python
def count_occurrences(tuple_of_elements, element):
    return tuple_of_elements.count(element)
# Test
my_tuple = (1, 2, 3, 2, 4, 2, 5)
print(count_occurrences(my_tuple, 2))  # Expected output: 3
```

Exercise 4.2.5:

```python
def merge_tuples(tuple1, tuple2):
    merge = tuple1 + tuple2
    return merge
# Test
tuple1 = (1, 2, 3)
tuple2 = (4, 5, 6)
print(merge_tuples(tuple1, tuple2))  # Expected output: (1, 2, 3, 4, 5, 6)
```

Exercise 4.2.6:

```python
def extract_subsequence(tuple_of_elements, start, end):
    return tuple_of_elements[start:end+1]
# Test
my_tuple = (1, 2, 3, 4, 5)
print(extract_subsequence(my_tuple, 1, 3))
# Expected output: (2, 3, 4)
```

4.2.3   Sets

Exercise 4.3.1

```python
def common_elements(set1, set2):
    return set1.intersection(set2)
# Test
set1 = {1, 2, 3, 4, 5}
set2 = {4, 5, 6, 7, 8}
print(common_elements(set1, set2))  # Expected output: {4, 5}
```

Exercise 4.3.2

```python
def unique_elements(set1, set2):
    return set1.union(set2)
# Test
set1 = {1, 2, 3, 4, 5}
set2 = {4, 5, 6, 7, 8}
print(unique_elements(set1, set2))  # Expected output: {1, 2, 3, 4, 5, 6, 7, 8}
```

Exercise 4.3.3

```python
def set_length(my_set):
    return len(my_set)
# Test
my_set = {1, 2, 3, 4, 5}
print(set_length(my_set))  # Expected output: 5
```

Exercise 4.3.4

```python
def set_difference(set1, set2):
    return set1.difference(set2)
# Test
set1 = {1, 2, 3, 4, 5}
set2 = {4, 5, 6, 7, 8}
print(set_difference(set1, set2))  # Expected output: {1, 2, 3}
```

Exercise 4.3.5

```python
def set_symmetric_difference(set1, set2):
    return set1.symmetric_difference(set2)
# Test
set1 = {1, 2, 3, 4, 5}
set2 = {4, 5, 6, 7, 8}
print(set_symmetric_difference(set1, set2))  # Expected output: {1, 2, 3, 6, 7, 8}
```

Exercise 4.3.6

```python
def is_subset(set1, set2):
    return set1.issubset(set2)
# Test
set1 = {1, 2, 3}
set2 = {1, 2, 3, 4, 5}
print(is_subset(set1, set2))  # Expected output: True
```

Chapter 5

Files

5 Files

5.1 Exercises

Exercise 5.1

Read the contents of a text file and display its content.

Exercise 5.2

Write text to a file.

Exercise 5.3

Count the number of lines in a file.

Exercise 5.4

Search for a word in a file and return the number of occurrences.

Exercise 5.5

Copy the contents of a source file to a destination file.

Exercise 5.6

Delete a file.

Exercise 5.7

Write a program that reads a CSV file containing information about students (name, age, grade) and displays the name of the student with the highest grade.

Exercise 5.8

Write a program that reads a CSV file containing information about employees (name, salary) and calculates the total sum of all employees' salaries.

Exercise 5.9

Write a program that reads a CSV file containing sales data (product, quantity, unit price) and calculates the total revenue.

Exercise 5.10

Write a program that reads a JSON file containing information about books (title, author, publication year) and displays the title of the most recent book.

Exercise 5.11

Write a program that reads a JSON file containing data about employees (name, age, department) and displays the name of the oldest employee.

Exercise 5.12

Write a program that reads a JSON file containing information about movies (title, director, duration) and displays the title of the longest movie.

Exercise 5.13

Write a program that reads a CSV file containing information about students (name, subject, grade) and creates a dictionary where the keys are the names of the students and the values are the averages of their grades.

Exercise 5.14

Write a program that reads a CSV file containing information about employees (name, department, salary) and creates an additional CSV file containing only the employees from the "Sales" department.

5.2 Correction

Exercise 5.1:

```python
filename = "my_file.txt"
with open(filename, 'r') as f:
    content = f.read()
print(content)
```

Exercise 5.2:

```python
filename = "my_file.txt"
text = "This is an example text."
with open(filename, 'w') as f:
    f.write(text)
```

Exercise 5.3:

```python
filename = "my_file.txt"
count = 0
with open(filename, 'r') as f:
    for line in f:
        count += 1
print(count)
```

Exercise 5.4:

```python
filename = "my_file.txt"
search_word = "example"
count = 0
with open(filename, 'r') as f:
    for line in f:
        words = line.split()
        count += words.count(search_word)
print(count)
```

Exercise 5.5:

```python
source = "source.txt"
destination = "destination.txt"
with open(source, 'r') as f1:
    content = f1.read()
with open(destination, 'w') as f2:
    f2.write(content)
```

Exercise 5.6:

```python
import os
filename = "my_file.txt"
if os.path.exists(filename):
    os.remove(filename)
    print(f"The file {filename} has been deleted.")
else:
    print(f"The file {filename} does not exist.")
```

Exercise 5.7:

```python
import csv
with open('students.csv', 'r') as file:
    reader = csv.reader(file)
    header = next(reader)
    best_grade = 0
    best_student = ""
    for row in reader:
        name, age, grade = row
        grade = float(grade)
        if grade > best_grade:
            best_grade = grade
            best_student = name
    print("The student with the highest grade is:", best_student)
```

Exercise 5.8:

```python
import csv
```

```python
total_salary = 0
with open('employees.csv', 'r') as file:
    reader = csv.reader(file)
    header = next(reader)
    for row in reader:
        name, salary = row
        salary = float(salary)
        total_salary += salary
print("The total sum of salaries is:", total_salary)
```

Exercise 5.9:

```python
import csv
total_revenue = 0
with open('sales.csv', 'r') as file:
    reader = csv.reader(file)
    header = next(reader)
    for row in reader:
        product, quantity, unit_price = row
        quantity = int(quantity)
        unit_price = float(unit_price)
        total_revenue += quantity * unit_price
print("The total revenue is:", total_revenue)
```

Exercise 5.10:

```python
import json
with open('books.json', 'r') as file:
    books = json.load(file)
    most_recent_book = max(books, key=lambda x: x['publication year'])
    print("The most recent book is:", most_recent_book['title'])
```

Exercise 5.11:

```python
import json
with open('employees.json', 'r') as file:
```

```python
    employees = json.load(file)
    oldest_employee = max(employees, key=lambda x: x['age'])
    print("The oldest employee is:", oldest_employee['name'])
```

Exercise 5.12:

```python
import json
with open('movies.json', 'r') as file:
    movies = json.load(file)
    longest_movie = max(movies, key=lambda x: x['duration'])
    print("The longest movie is:", longest_movie['title'])
```

Exercise 5.13:

```python
import csv
average_grades = {}
with open('students.csv', 'r') as file:
    reader = csv.reader(file)
    header = next(reader)
    for row in reader:
        name, subject, grade = row
        grade = float(grade)
        if name in average_grades:
            average_grades[name].append(grade)
        else:
            average_grades[name] = [grade]
for name, grades in average_grades.items():
    average = sum(grades) / len(grades)
    average_grades[name] = average
print("Averages of students' grades:", average_grades)
```

Exercise 5.14:

```python
import csv
sales_employees = []
with open('employees.csv', 'r') as file:
```

```python
    reader = csv.reader(file)
    header = next(reader)
    for row in reader:
        name, department, salary = row
        if department == "Sales":
            sales_employees.append([name, department, salary])
with open('sales_employees.csv', 'w', newline='') as file:
    writer = csv.writer(file)
    writer.writerow(header)
    writer.writerows(sales_employees)
print("The file for 'Sales' department employees has been created successfully.")
```

Chapter 6

Recursion

6 Recursion

6.1 Exercises

Exercise 6.1:

Write the recursive function that calculates the sum of the first n integers.

Exercise 6.2:

Write a recursive function that calculates the sum $1+1/2+1/3+\cdots+1/n$.

Exercise 6.3:

Provide a recursive function that calculates the sum of the digits of an integer n.

Exercise 6.4:

Using exercise 3, give the recursive function that checks if an integer is divisible by 3.

Hint: An integer is divisible by 3 if the sum of its digits is divisible by 3.

Exercise 6.5:

Give the recursive function that calculates the Fibonacci sequence.

The Fibonacci sequence is defined as follows:

$U0=1$

$U1=1$

$Un=Un-1+Un-2$

Exercise 6.6:

Provide the recursive function that calculates x^n.

6.2 Correction

Exercise 6.1:

```
def recursive_sum_of_integers(n):
    if n == 0:
        return 0
    else:
        return n + recursive_sum_of_integers(n-1)
# Test
print(recursive_sum_of_integers(5))  # Expected output: 15
```

Exercise 6.2:

```
def recursive_sum_of_fractions(n):
    if n == 1:
        return 1
    else:
        return 1/n + recursive_sum_of_fractions(n-1)
# Test
print(recursive_sum_of_fractions(5))  # Expected output: 2.283333333333333
```

Exercise 6.3:

```
def recursive_sum_of_digits(n):
    if n < 10:
        return n
    else:
        return n % 10 + recursive_sum_of_digits(n // 10)
# Test
print(recursive_sum_of_digits(12345))  # Expected output: 15
```

Exercise 6.4:

```
def recursive_divisible_by_three(n):
    if n < 10:
        return n % 3 == 0
```

```python
    else:
        return (n % 10 + recursive_divisible_by_three(n // 10)) % 3 == 0
# Test
print(recursive_divisible_by_three(12345))  # Expected output: True
print(recursive_divisible_by_three(987654321))  # Expected output: False
```

Exercise 6.5:

```python
def recursive_fibonacci(n):
    if n <= 1:
        return n
    else:
        return recursive_fibonacci(n-1) + recursive_fibonacci(n-2)
# Test
print(recursive_fibonacci(6))  # Expected output: 8
```

Exercise 6.6:

```python
def recursive_calculate_xn(x, n):
    if n == 0:
        return 1
    elif n % 2 == 0:
        return recursive_calculate_xn(x * x, n // 2)
    else:
        return x * recursive_calculate_xn(x * x, n // 2)
# Test
print(recursive_calculate_xn(2, 4))  # Expected output: 16
```

Chapter 7

Practice exercise (Data Structures)

7 Practice exercise (Data structures)

7.1 Exercise

Exercise 7.1

Consider a dictionary that contains informations about a student: student ID, name, first name, and field of study.

1) Provide the function to input a list of n students.

2) Provide a function to display a list of students.

3) Provide a function to assign the information of one student to another student.

4) Provide a function to swap the information of two students.

5) Write the function to add a student at the beginning of the list.

   The function takes the list of students and the information of the student to be added as parameters.

6) Write the function to remove a student.

   The function takes the list of students, the name, and the first name of the student to be removed as parameters.

7) Provide a function to search for a student by their name and first name.

8) Provide a function to sort a list of students by their name and first name.

9) Write a menu that allows calling the above operations.

7.2 Correction

Exercise 7.1:

```python
# 1) Enter a list of n students
def input_students(n):
    students = []
    for i in range(n):
        student = {}
        student["student_id"] = input("Student ID: ")
        student["last_name"] = input("Last Name: ")
        student["first_name"] = input("First Name: ")
        student["major"] = input("Major: ")
        students.append(student)
    return students


# 2) Display a list of students
def display_students(students):
    for student in students:
        print("Student ID:", student["student_id"])
        print("Last Name:", student["last_name"])
        print("First Name:", student["first_name"])
        print("Major:", student["major"])
        print()


# 3) Assign the information of one student to another student
def assign_information(dest_student, src_student):
    dest_student["student_id"] = src_student["student_id"]
    dest_student["last_name"] = src_student["last_name"]
    dest_student["first_name"] = src_student["first_name"]
    dest_student["major"] = src_student["major"]


# 4) Swap the information of two students
```

```python
def swap_information(student1, student2):
    temp = student1.copy()
    assign_information(student1, student2)
    assign_information(student2, temp)


# 5) Add a student at the beginning of the list
def add_student_at_beginning(students_list, student):
    students_list.insert(0, student)


# 6) Remove a student
def remove_student(students_list, last_name, first_name):
    for student in students_list:
        if student["last_name"] == last_name and student["first_name"] == first_name:
            students_list.remove(student)
            break


# 7) Search for a student by their last name and first name
def search_student(students_list, last_name, first_name):
    for student in students_list:
        if student["last_name"] == last_name and student["first_name"] == first_name:
            return student
    return None


# 8) Sort a list of students by their last name and first name
def sort_students(students):
    return sorted(students, key=lambda x: (x["last_name"], x["first_name"]))


# 9) Menu to call the operations
def menu():
    students_list = []
    while True:
        print("\n----- MENU -----")
        print("1. Enter a list of students")
```

```python
    print("2. Display the list of students")
    print("3. Assign the information of one student to another student")
    print("4. Swap the information of two students")
    print("5. Add a student at the beginning of the list")
    print("6. Remove a student")
    print("7. Search for a student")
    print("8. Sort the list of students")
    print("9. Quit")
    choice = int(input("Choice: "))
    if choice == 1:
        n = int(input("Number of students: "))
        students_list = input_students(n)
    elif choice == 2:
        display_students(students_list)
    elif choice == 3:
        dest_student = {"student_id": "", "last_name": "", "first_name": "", "major": ""}
        src_student = {"student_id": "123", "last_name": "Smith", "first_name": "John",
"major": "Computer Science"}
        assign_information(dest_student, src_student)
        print(dest_student)
    elif choice == 4:
        student1 = {"student_id": "123", "last_name": "Smith", "first_name": "John", "major":
"Computer Science"}
        student2 = {"student_id": "456", "last_name": "Doe", "first_name": "Jane", "major":
"Mathematics"}
        swap_information(student1, student2)
        print(student1)
        print(student2)
    elif choice == 5:
        student = {"student_id": "789", "last_name": "Johnson", "first_name": "Emily",
"major": "Physics"}
        add_student_at_beginning(students_list, student)
    elif choice == 6:
```

```python
            last_name = input("Last Name of the student to remove: ")
            first_name = input("First Name of the student to remove: ")
            remove_student(students_list, last_name, first_name)
        elif choice == 7:
            last_name = input("Last Name of the student to search: ")
            first_name = input("First Name of the student to search: ")
            student = search_student(students_list, last_name, first_name)
            if student:
                print(student)
            else:
                print("Student not found.")
        elif choice == 8:
            students_list = sort_students(students_list)
        elif choice == 9:
            break
        else:
            print("Invalid choice. Please try again.")
# Call the menu function to test the operations
menu()
```